NEUTRAL

a poem by

BILL SHUTE

Kendra Steiner Editions #420

Composed May 2021-July 2022

Thanks to Mary Anne Bernal

In Memory of
Frank Samperi
Gianfranco Parolini
Lee Konitz
& Pat Boyette

kendrasteinereditions.wordpress.com

"Silence is my substitute for counterpoint"

--Morton Feldman

"...any form of running away from *what is* creates dependence..."

--J. Krishnamurti

NEUTRAL

riding the waves for a week

in a collage-artist's loft

overloooking the Yazoo River

between the Veterans Hospital

& the beauty parlor

kept afloat

by wavering bass clarinet

& harmonium

not knowing the backstory,

we projected our own

onto the scene

ears sculpted

from sandstone

unmeasured, but not unmeasurable

betrayed
by sight

familiar with
the bird

but not
its name

in the shade
of the sun

even the ghosts
carry guns

should I cut the pills
in half
and take them daily
or take an entire pill
every other day?

power-washing
the sunrise sidewalks

orienting my self
by the clatter
of the pallets

being loaded
onto the river barges

cartoony murals
in the alley,

wake-up calls
from a few years back

pork rinds & kissyfaces

once taken
for granted,
now
out of reach

walking zen

not

sitting zen

stacks of business card-sized

sheets of dried & smoked

Korean seaweed

fueling me

for another morning-after

matter and mind

mid-stream

knowing when
to hang up the cleats
& move
to the front office

& survive
on the smiles
of strangers

believing
we've found
the path
around
the statues
of eternity

a half-block
down
to the shore

how shallow
the steps

how steep
the incline

they didn't realize
he could speak

until he spoke
up

within
my sight

but

beyond
my grasp

through

a place,

through

a project

the grey,

the chill,

the vacuum

before the next storm

lights out   for magic words

aged in bourbon barrels

forming vertical teams

of communications welders

too busy defining

& requiring excellence

to attend

to the details

one   fades out

another   fades in

in watermelon weather

goose skirts
convenience fees
and mold that sparkles

required to agree
that the evaluation

was not
an evaluation

but a dialogue

one half

of my self

critiquing

the other

more smoke

than fire

heads
with faces
not visible

the chairs provided
are handsome

but cut off
circulation to our legs

no fresh fruit or vegetables
at the competing dollar-stores
where we score our groceries

setting
rat traps
in rooms
where I am
afraid to sleep

reminded to not wake
the Royal baby

yellow squash
okra
& tomatoes
from the backyard garden

watching the sun rise
through a cracked washateria window

liars
in a strange
rainy world

tired,

but graceful

between in-crowds

and old feelings

the intervals,

the spaces

stain

upon

stain

no one

could explain

how to get to

the island across the river

or so says

the Coffee-Drinkin' Nighthawk,

overnight voice

out of WWVA,

Wheeling, West Virginia

monitoring the flashes
inside & outside
during the crimson
& elastic evenings

assassins
dressed as clowns

details can be inserted
later
to justify
their conclusions

the upscale law office
was constructed around
two abandoned rowboats
as no one wanted to
move them

waltzing
around the pyramid
of forms
unable to find
an entrance

he'd had
everything
but lost
more

Marcia labelled herself
a Platonist
and labelled me
an Aristotelian

turtles whose shells
had evaporated

sealing my experience
in a shadowbox

whatever the situation

under review,

Thomas would interject

one of the 210 explanations

for the fall of the Roman Empire

he'd memorized,

his tone suggesting

that the application & relevance

of each

was self-evident

extinguished candles

expired user ID's

eyes sculpted

from sandstone

access granted

to the roof

and the basement

the mood lighting
never turns off,
even when
we sleep

steeped in beforeness
coated in not-yet-ness

no clocks
& few right angles
on the casino floor

selling bridges
they don't own

lines of sight
theories of sleep

this year's snake oil

rough
idling

nuance
and scruple

matter
and mind

held together

by mortar

mixed and set

seven generations ago

the silver balloon
we'd released
up to Heaven
for our departed colleague
drifted back to the ground
in the next town over
out of our sight

cleansing
plum rains

having assembled
an intentional family

air castles

interruptions

broken hints

on the job,

but no longer

on the payroll

olive oil

fennel seed

white pepper

& dried potato flakes

not the same

and yet

not another

speeding
on the highway to
one more than what we need

intertwined
with iron-poor blood
with the blessing
of the Duke of Norwich

while our sinks
are backed-up
full of used dishwater

the last day
we can still argue that
the dirty laundry is clean
and convince anyone
beyond ourselves

not able
to concentrate

absorbed
into the spectacle

the previous resident
left behind
childhood beach photos &
wedding decorations
which had been repurposed
as coasters & bookends

weighing
the breeze-blown preferences
from sledgehammers
to soufflés

chasing one high
after another

debating between
labelling the newest literary creation
translation or paraphrase

what the riverboat casino's gumbo
lacked in flavor,

the diners and servers
lacked in enthusiasm

across Washington Street
a limping cat
sniffs the empty sidewalk,
eventually licking it

too many years
without a Spring

what we perceived
to be melody
evaporated
before we could trap it
in our nets

noon church bells

arrive

before the storm

they sang of a "moonbeam haze"

in a corner, near the kitchen,

for tips

& a salad per person

pipes that had burst

during the February freeze

& power outage

waiting in perfumed chambers,

gazing   on vacancy

down to the last few grains
in the egg-timer

no longer youthful,
but still juvenile

they sampled
others' suffering
as if
sampling an Islay Scotch
they could not afford

the groundskeeper
works overtime
to afford
celebrity tequilas

sealing my experience
in a shadowbox

between in-crowds
& old feelings

waltzing
around the pyramid
of forms
unable to find
an entrance

they interpreted
his nervous tics
as intended gestures

while his mother prayed
for a cleansing
snowfall

from the Rust Belt
to the Gulf Coast

re-roasting   the tea

channeling others' voices

isolated   but surrounded

self-identifying
by which of the stopped clocks
we choose
to observe

pauses

and skips

and replays

in our internal narratives

on the track,
but no longer
part of the race

solar energy
mined into data
with market value

or so the theorists of regulation
have observed

four clay tea jars

unglazed,
    able to
        breathe

within
    my sight

        but

beyond
    my grasp

as moonlight

as water

outside

the Divine milieu

unmeasured,

but not

unmeasurable

they worked hard
        at appearing
                inattentive

as we step over   and around
the clutter of products
they'd gone into debt for
    but now   left behind

speed bumps
    yield signs
        & tax liens

smelling of lavender body wash
        & cedar closets

her sister is
        a visual artist & filmmaker
        specializing in depictions
            of drunkenness & dissipation

in this village
    with no corners
        or sidewalks

matter

and mind

tumbles

and leaps

resting

over the 30-minute lunch break

on a bench

formed from recycled tires

between a framing shop

&

a now-vacant bookstore

cuts and scrapes

on my arms & legs

that I can't explain

or remember getting

he'd had everything

but lost more

advised to amplify

the vegetal notes

in the afternoon's oolong blend

vanity metrics

&

carbohydrate-filled clouds

continuing   on

when the flagstones end

shotgun-shacks

and melting raspberry sno-cones

gild the lily,

geld the horse

only the floors
the ceilings
and the fourth walls

offer escape,
transcendence

we never knew
what the train carried
or why—
and never considered
inquiring

found wanting

when measured against
brushed stainless steel

cowering
to the cosmic tyrant
they'd created
in their own image

on the job,
but no longer
on the payroll

rainwater
half-fills the lightbulbs
intended to illuminate
the walkway
to the afterlife

not the same

and yet
not another

reminded

the meter

was still

running

saving
my last clean shirt

for an event
I can't anticipate

multiple periods & cultures
tossed into the blender
for a phenomena smoothie

the particulars
blended away

This week rainy and cool, a welcome change,
For me, but once again washing away
Enthusiasm from the locals, who
Drink and bicker and drive too long for
Such short distances. Without wheels I walk
A mile or so in each direction,
After sunrise, at sundown, rain or not,
A stowaway on someone else's cruise.

Seasonal workers housed in groups on the
Floor above me, unanswered cell phones
Chiming -- painting and landscaping crews not
Able to work in the rain drink warm three-
Dollar six-packs and argue about how
To bet on this weekend's Rangers games. Rain.

no one would speak
until
I signed
the confidentiality agreement

creamy-white
sand crystals
drop through
the hourglass

struggling
to re-gain
balance

shaving away

the dead skin

from my heels

more rapid

than the falcon

the intervals,

the spaces

marinated
    in malt liquor

someone else
    holds the key
        to the padlock
    on the storage shed
on this property

self-identifying
    by which constant
        in the riverfront drone
        we choose
    to tune our instruments by

another sunrise

another blank page

to be filled with

both

activity & indolence

one

fades out

the other

fades in

settling in

as a guest   on a ship

piloted by those born

a few generations later

the fireflies

avoid the potted plants

nothing   other

than   the now

no longer standing on tip-toes
to see beyond
the vernacular

as the next teams
gather to take
the field

nothing
that a pint
of Community Coffee
& a link of seafood baudin
won't cure

midstream

preferably, without

vibrato

guided by

imagined daystars,

unclaimed by

the rental economy

fascinated

at the cleverness

of the beast,

which does not

defeat or destroy

itself -- instead

melting into

inaccessible crevices

& unnoticed cracks

once taken
for granted
now
out of reach

how shallow
the steps

how steep
the decline

a concerned crow

atop a chalk-stained chimney

cries out with excitement

and urgency

and the others react

and all depart

within

my sight

but beyond

my grasp

short-sleeved
transparency

in need of an understated
oboe & celeste accompaniment

reclaiming
the time
and effort
spent arguing
with the tides

betrayed

by sight

when the rain

does not cancel

out the sun

unmeasured,

but not

unmeasurable

++++++++++++++++++++++++++++++

MORE POETRY FROM BILL SHUTE:

LOCKDOWN CORRESPONDENCES

DOWN AND OUT IN GULFPORT & BILOXI

BRIDGE ON THE BAYOU

POINT LOMA PURPLE

TWELVE GATES TO THE CITY

SCULPTURE GARDEN IN THE SNOW

SATORI IN NATCHEZ

NO BRICKS, NO TEMPLES

AMONG THE NEWLY FALLEN

RIVERSIDE FUGUE

APPROACHING THE APPARENT (w/ David Payne)

CULTURE OF COMPLIANCE (w/ Michael Casey)

and from Moloko Print (Germany):

JUNK SCULPTURE FROM THE NEW GILDED AGE:
SELECTED POEMS, 2005-2017

kendrasteinereditions.wordpress.com

www.ingramcontent.com/pod-product-compliance
Lightning Source LLC
LaVergne TN
LVHW090046160826
845672LV00015B/1587